DUTIES OF GRANDPARENTS

Torkom Saraydarian

T.S.G.
PUBLISHING FOUNDATION, INC.

Duties of Grandparents

ISBN: 0-929874-60-9

Library of Congress Catalog Card Number: 96-61709

Printed in the United States of America

Printed by: *KNI, Incorporated*
Anaheim, CA 92806

Published by: **T.S.G. Publishing Foundation, Inc.**
P.O. Box 7068
Cave Creek, AZ 85331-7068
United States of America

Duties of Grandparents

When I wrote *Sex, Family, and the Woman in Society,* regarding family relationships, I missed talking about grandparents. The grandparents and parents are very important. They are the mechanism in the evolution of humanity. That is a very important thing to say. To be parents, to raise children is a spiritual, magnificent, and special mechanism. It is not two, three people, but it is the hands of evolution. It is a great tool to enhance, to promote the evolution of humanity.

Grandparents are not old shoes who have finished their job, to be put on shelves or sent to different places. Grandparents have their special role in evolution. Without them the evolution, the progress of humanity, will not proceed in the best ways. They have a great role to play in family life, in social life, everywhere, if they know their role and how to manage their role in the family.

First of all I believe that parents stand for the present. It is very strange that parents teach the children the present values: competition, schools, colleges, universities, how to make money, how to buy houses, properties, how to make their life pleasant and beautiful. They stand for the present.

I have watched many, many parents, and they do the same thing. They are concerned with their children's dressing, schooling, behavior, and their relationships with daily events. They are concerned with how to manage their children and how to protect them. This is very interesting.

Grandparents stand for the future. They inspire the children in the real values of life because they passed through that experience of being young and beautiful and rich and pleasant. They passed the life of pleasures. Now they are seventy, eighty, they have cooled down, and they know really what life is. Parents do not know that. Parents are very happy now, strong, healthy; they teach health and happiness to their children. But grandparents know what the suffering of life is, what pain and suffering are, what is sickness, how many times they faced death. They conversed with death and took special wisdom from the experience of meeting death. It is a very valuable cycle.

If they accumulate lots of wisdom, they slowly pass it to their grandchildren, but in such a balanced way that the balance is not distorted. The present and the future will be balanced with such a dosage of wisdom that the children do not lose their present and do not neglect their future.

Now I decided to divide this topic into eight parts, but they are not commands, not orders, not laws. These are experiences which you can use or throw out.

1. Grandparents must teach their grandchildren the real values of life, of course in a balanced dosage. The children must know that day and night playing football, basketball, and coming home tired, or going to parties, drinking, and doping are not real values. But they are values to the children. How to talk to the children with such a wisdom that does not negate their assumed values? Grandparents will put new wisdom into children's minds in such a way that slowly they see the transience of what

they are doing in life. Five hours, ten hours of playing football and tennis or running after girls or boys, swimming day and night — it is good for them because that is what their nature wants. But Grandpa, Grandma will gather them and tell them about different values in such a way that does not distort the balance. There is a very tricky way.

You do not say, "Do not play football," but you say, "There are different values. Look at life this way." You do this with stories, with parables, with deep wisdom, intelligence. We are not talking about hobo grandparents. We are talking about the grandparents who are intelligent, live together fifty years, eighty years. They did not divorce every five years. Grandparents are such a mechanism in the evolution. You must see their value. Many, many great men or women in the history of humanity were made to sit by their grandparents, who would kiss them and whisper these few words to them that go eternally in their minds as a shining light: "We love you. We think about your future."

Actually, in parenthesis we can say that to be grandparents is an honor, is a graduation from life, is an emancipation from the transient values of life. It leads from the unreal to the real. They eventually know that life is real, but not real. It is so beautiful to mix that together and present it to the children so that they do not get frustrated in their lives.

I know a grand lady who asked me one day, "When are you going to come to your senses?" I laughed and escaped from her. Then I went under a pine tree and sat there and asked myself, "What did she say to me?" She asked, "When are you coming to your senses?" My hobby was to climb the trees and go to the top and shake myself, left and right. It was so pleasant to me. Many times I fell, I know. I thought and thought that now I am going to come to my senses. Eventually I went back and asked, "What do you mean?" She said, "You are living like a monkey in trees, rivers, oceans. What is it? Don't you have a focus?" "Focus, what is focus?" I asked. She was opening Infinity in me. The finite is slowly mixing with the Infinite. I asked, "What is focus?" She replied, "Focus is a goal or a purpose that you stick to and eventually actualize." That day my life changed. My consciousness shifted from one level to another level. I said, "I did not know that there was such a level of thinking." Now that day I started to be serious with life.

Now the first duty of the grandparent is to create focus, nothing else. "Come baby. Let us play a game." They play a game, then eat many unhealthy things. You are not a grandparent. A grandparent is supposed to be a way leading grandchildren to the future, whatever that future is in the grandparent's mind. But it is at least a future. Whoever failed in his grandparency has really failed. Grandparents must be so careful that they play their role.

For example, we have a big machine. Your role is to supervise this part. The parent's role is to supervise that part, other parts. Now are you playing your role? If you play your role nicely, they will play their role nicely. It is a different approach. It is very scientific. It is very evolutionary.

Those children who do not have grandparents for some reason are karmically deprived, unless in a special arrangement they are taken away from their grandparents' influence to be helped differently for a specific role which they will play in life.

This is also the case for grandparents. They are forbidden the care of their grandchildren because of their mental and emotional attitude. Do not forget that the Guardian Angels of little ones prearranged all the relationships for the progress of the little one, or for a temporary retribution because of his past karma.

Ideal grandparents are the product of many incarnations until they meet the requirements to be a guidance for little ones. Of course, little ones also must have past karma available to be under the guidance of ideal grandparents, to be under their light and have access to the treasury of their experiences.

Sometimes a child has grandparents, but the child is thrown to them as a burden. For karmic reasons the grandparents will not give the needed guidance but will be very hard or indifferent to the grandchild. This kind of phenomenon suggests to us that there are karmic webs working eventually to bring a better relationship.

2. The second duty of grandparents is slowly to introduce them to the Other Worlds. The trauma of children is very, very great. It puts a wound in their psyche to such a depth that the children cannot overcome it in the future — that shock when their parents die, their grandparents die, a friend dies, somebody dies. They are in great shock because when they are children, they believe they will be happy forever. Grandparents sneakily, nicely, wisely will show them that everything decays in the Universe. Grandparents will be sick and die. "Grandma, I do not want you to die." "That is the law of Nature. As the birth is beautiful, the death will be glorious." "Really?" Now the seeds are planted. "You know, Grandma one day will die." "Really?" "I do not want you to die." "If we do not die, we do not *come back* with beautiful bodies and more advanced mechanisms."

Now what you are doing is shifting the consciousness of the children and preparing them to face the calamities or beauties of life. Then you say, "Mommy will die one day." "Mommy? Mommy are you going to die one day?" "Who knows?" she answers, because parents are for the present. "Daddy, Grandma said you are going to die." "Oh, Grandma is sick." Look what parents are doing. They are not keeping the balance.

Then Grandma will show that the dogs and cats will die, the trees will die, the flowers will die, and they will be born again, regenerate again. A new beauty will come and go, will come and go, will come and go. Now the child is ready. When his Mommy dies, he does not have that trauma. He does not have that psychic wound that goes forever. It is so beautiful to prepare children for the transience of every form, but gradually, like a game, without causing shock to the consciousness of the children.

Grandma takes a dead flower and says, "The flower died, but a new flower will come. Every living form will go through the death and birth processes."

The little one will gather wisdom, which will help him or her in future calamities.

3. The third thing the grandparents are going to teach the children is seclusion and retreat. This is very important for their life, especially when their love-life starts, marriage starts, engagement starts, as there are great traumas there. They must work on it and say, "You must sometimes for two minutes try to be lonely, to be by yourself." "Yes, what will it do, Grandma?" "You think differently and see things nicer. You live. You feel your own presence." Many people do not live their own presence. In solitude you meet your Self, of course in advanced stages.

When I am saying these words, they are on a scale of one to one hundred. You must make them gradient and gradually give them to the children. If they learn to stay lonely, isolated, secluded, in retreat for ten minutes, one hour, two hours, they will not tell you, "I am lonely," because some Presence in them will communicate with them. The Guardian Angel, in which maybe you believe or you do not believe, will communicate with them, especially if they are below the age of seven. At that time they are still in the Higher Worlds. They know these things, but the present problems, pain and suffering, and hunger block them. The child is blocked at seven, eight, nine years old, but even then you can open the Higher Worlds in them.

I remember my parents left me alone when as a child I was talking with invisible people. They were my friends, but Mommy did not see them. She asked, "What is happening to you?" Daddy said, "Leave him alone. Do not interrupt him." I used to play with the friends. At three, four, five years old, they were there. They were with me. I do not need any proof, so the Other World is still with me. If you want to read about this, read *Other Worlds*. It is all based on my experiences.

Slowly, slowly, Grandpa is going to inject into the consciousness of the children that there is another world toward which we are preparing ourselves. "All the life, from babyhood until my age, even at eighty-five, ninety, is a preparation to enter into those glories." "What, Grandpa?" "Glories." "How come?" "It is a glorious world. You are free from your body, from your emotional body, from your mental body — freedom." Only very advanced and spiritual and intellectual people can evaluate and appreciate such a release from life. This story must be told to the children in fables, in myths, in legends.

Grandma, Grandpa have great things to do. They prepare themselves when grandchildren are coming to them for a week. "What will I do? I know what to do. I will take them here, take them there. Let them have fun! What is that fun? It is fun." Instead of that, Grandma will think what kind of stories she must tell to lead their little, little steps to the Other Worlds in a very nice, mild way so that they will be interested more and more and come to their Grandma and ask, "What exists in the Other Worlds?" "All our friends that passed away are there. Great Ones are there. Great symphonies of color and music are there. Great thought waves and currents and magnificent energies that created all this Universe are in the Other Worlds." Can you imagine such a grandparent? We are creating the ideal in your vision so that you work on it.

4. The fourth duty or obligation of grandparents is to familiarize the children with visualization. There were grandparents that I used to visit with their grandchildren because, unfortunately, my grandparents were massacred. They were butchered in the Armenian genocide. I did not understand until now that I searched for grandparents to sit and learn with their grandchildren. Those special grandparents said, "Now let us close our eyes. Let us visualize a rose." It was such fun. I started to see a rose. I was surprised, shocked. I was seeing it with closed eyes; then the other children saw it. Then Grandpa said, "Let us change the rose into a chrysanthemum." I had a little difficulty but I did it. Then eventually, eventually, eventually three, four months later he said, "Let us be a rosebush." It was very difficult to dis-identify with this body and be something else, but I did it. These are things that I learned not in books but by experience, from great people like that Grandma, Grandpa who taught to their grandchildren visualization.

Immediately when grandchildren come to visit, they open the refrigerator and everything nasty for their health is in that refrigerator. "Here in my pocket are the bonbons. Here, eat!" Oh, children devour that, and Grandma is so happy that children are eating poison because she is ignorant.

Grandparents must have a preparation to handle their grandchildren, how to approach them, how to talk with them in a gradient scale so that they do not distort also the children's "reality."

Visualization, when developed, becomes a door toward "continuity of consciousness," and children from a young age are emancipated from the fear of death in any form.

5. Grandparents must teach children also how to detach and eventually to destroy their ego, vanity, and self-interest. This is supreme. They will not learn this in our universities. Our universities will teach to have ego, vanity, and competition so that they step on the heads of others to be successful. It is so tragic, but Grandma will teach them. "It was not nice to beat that boy and take his toys from his hands." "Why Grandma?" "It was very selfish, it was very egotistical, it was vanity because you thought you were something. You did it. The poor boy cried, suffered, and went home. Look what you did." Who is going to teach that? You? Who is going to put those seeds that ego, vanity, selfishness are the highest cancers in the world — psychic cancers. Physical cancers are good in some way, but psychic cancers live with you for ages and incarnations, and you cannot get rid of them. Those greedy people who devastate the life, greedy groups, greedy nations, greedy governments that are devastating the life of the planet, the health of the planet, are those people whose Grandmas did not teach them to get rid of ego, vanity, and selfishness. It is so beautiful.

Grandparents must gradually teach how to be noble, to recognize the right and dignity of other children, and to have a relationship which is not based on ego and vanity. Such a child will be free from the worst enemies living within him.

6. The sixth duty is very beautiful. It is to teach the grandchildren to be honest, to be direct, not to deceive and lie. Many women, many men, forty, fifty years old still slander, deceive, and lie in such a dirty way that you cannot imagine because they never learned that honesty is

better than dishonesty. Truth is more pro-survival than lying. If you want to survive, to prosper, stay in the truth. Do not change things. Do not deceive and then hide under the blankets. It is so dirty. Who is going to teach this? Mommy will not teach this. "How did you get that little knife in your pocket, Charley?" "Oh, I stole it." "From whom?" "From Johnny." "Oh, it is so bad." "Why, Grandma?" You may open the doors of the Law of Karma even — that whatever you did for others, others will do the same for you. You teach them to be noble, beautiful, shining, and they will shine with such beautiful health.

I had six hundred children in a school. I watched them, observed them. Those who were sneaky, those who were liars, those who followed deceit, slander, and so on were not healthy, absolutely! Their psychic mechanism was crooked, and those children who were honest, open, frank, beautiful, direct, shone with their energy and vigor.

What I am talking about are pro-survival techniques. There is no mysticism here. There is no metaphysics. It is life, and who is going to do that? It is not the Mommy. Mommy is too busy in the office, and when she comes from the office she throws off her dress and tries to prepare some dinner, and after dinner she is so tired she must go to bed. Who is going to talk with the children? They are waiting for the parents; and the man is coming and opening the refrigerator and taking a big beer, second beer, third beer. "How are you doing my children? Hi. Go to sleep or watch TV." This is the average house.

So the honesty, the nobility of the children must be protected from an early age so that they become healthy, really healthy. Many diseases will not enter into them because their electromagnetic aura is organized by nobility and honesty.

7. Grandma and Grandpa will slowly give the grandchildren the mood, the consciousness, the awareness to

be joyful in life. It is very tricky; it is very valuable; it needs great wisdom to tell children how to be really joyful, how to harness joy from flowers, beautiful faces, friends, from the trees, from the rivers, how to be grateful, how to be joyful in life; and Grandpa will find every minute to present an object of joy. Children must be charged with joy. "Joy is a special wisdom," says the Great Sage, and joy is a healthy aura. It is so important.

In the beginning, the children must try to find opportunities or objects or subjects to gather joy from them. For example, if their friend was successful in the class, they will not be jealous. They will say, "Oh I am so happy my friend did it." If somebody is dressing better than her, she will be thrilled that that girl is dressing better than her. Do you understand this consciousness which is not here yet, not anywhere? These kinds of values must be introduced to the life, that that girl is playing tennis and I am playing tennis with her. She won. "Oh, you did it. You are my ideal," or you can say, "Son of a gun, I lost it. I will show him next time," and next time you become worse because you are poisoned by your own poison. Do you understand such kind of things? I am just planting seeds in your mind. If you become grandparents in the next life, you will come to your senses and not live like hobos.

There are grandparents who are like little children. I was reading the other day the senior citizens' magazine. I said, "What is this? They are all writing how to make more money, how to have more fun, how to take more vacations. They are not thinking how to prepare themselves for dying." It is such a degenerated state of consciousness that at eighty-nine, ninety still he is banking, making money. To whom are you going to give that money? What are you going to do with it? Money, money! It is a sickness. Think about your values. How you are going to face your Angel? How you are going to face your Master? Our seniors are like little children. They are playing dominoes. They are playing cards, sitting there in the old folks' home. I visited there. I asked, "What are you doing?" "We are playing cards," as if playing cards will lead them to their destination.

When opportunity and honor are given to you to be a Grandma or Grandpa, accept this wisdom. You are a tool, a mechanism in the big mechanism of evolution. You can play your role or escape from your role. Many Grandpas, Grandmas leave their grandchildren because they are headaches. Why? It is because the children are keeping them from their card games, parties, drinking, and so on. They go to the other side of the world so as not to see their grandchildren. They are escaping from themselves, which is impossible.

In any opportunity, the grandparents must make their grandchildren joyful, not happy, but joyful. Accumulated joy in their aura can fight against diseases in the future. Accumulated joy in their nature can prevent them from falling into vices. They must create every opportunity to feel joy from flowers, from trees, from mountains, from rivers, even to such a degree that through joy they become ecstatic. Such children will be healthy and, even if karma leads them to difficult situations, they will have someone in their life to guide them.

Joy will be the oil in all their public relations and prevent any hard friction.

8. The eighth one is that Grandma and Grandpa are going to discipline intelligently, psychologically, beautifully and make the grandchildren serve. "Go wash these dishes. Clean this room. Iron this." "Oh Grandma, I came here for fun." "That is the fun!" If you teach the children to serve, they will be magnificent.

Grandparents must cultivate in the grandchildren a drive to serve their parents, their neighbors, other children without expectation and with great joy.

Service rendered without expectation naturally helps them eventually to realize their Self and makes them a magnetic person for generations to come.

Q & A

Question: *What role does the godparent play in regard to the grandchildren?*

Answer: Godparents are the same as grandparents if the children do not have grandparents. It is a Christian tradition that if anything happens, godparents are there if the godparents know their role. It is a ritual in the church but no instructions are given. "You are becoming a godparent. Do you know what you are going to do?" This is it. They must be instructed and trained.

Question: *Are the suggestions the same if the grandchild lives with the grandparents?*

Answer: Yes. Grandparents and parents have the same roles in different layers. They must not contradict each other. That is why sometimes when grandparents speak to their children, wife and husband, they reorient them in certain levels so that the parents do not deal with their children in a way that opposes the grandparents' teaching. It is a mutual communication, intercommunication, and that is what the beauty of family is.

In our home, you will not believe if I tell you, our home was so big that on the roof there was a hall, and in that hall at noon and every night, two hundred people would sit and eat. Who were the two hundred people? They were grandparents, children, children's children, husbands and wives. Grandma and Grandpa ruled the table and would say, "Let us pray. Let us eat." As far as I remember, in that home there were no disputes. With every little problem that arose they would go to the supreme psychologist, who was Grandma, and she would say, "Do not do that. Do this. Do you understand?" "Yes." There was no problem.

In the future, people will turn to the survival way, the traditional way, and live together under one roof.

Index

C

Children
  and death, 5
  and Higher Worlds, 6

D

Death, 2
Discipline, 12

E

Ego, vanity
  how taught about, 9

F

Focus, 4

G

Grandparents
  and evolution, 1
  and future, 2
  as an honor, 3
Grandparents,
  not having, 4
Grandparents, ideal, 4
Guardian Angel, 6
Guardian Angels, 4

H

Health
  and honesty, 10
Honesty
  how taught, 9

J

Joy and health, 12
Joy in life, 10

K

Karma, 4

L

Law of Karma, 10

O

Other Worlds, 5, 7

P

Parents
  and present time, 1
Psychic cancers, 9

S

Self, 12
  how explained, 6
Senior citizens
  and values, 11
Service, 12
Solitude
  how to teach, 6
Story:
  Of T.S. and old lady/
  focus, 3

V

Values, real, 2
Visualization, 8

About the Author

This booklet is the transcription of a lecture by Torkom Saraydarian given in 1996.

The author's books have been used all over the world as sources of guidance and inspiration in living a life based on the teachings of the Ageless Wisdom. Some of the books have been translated into other languages, including Armenian, German, Dutch, Danish, Portuguese, French, Spanish, Italian, Greek, Yugoslavian, and Swedish. The author holds lectures and seminars in the United States as well as in other parts of the world.

Torkom Saraydarian's entire life has been a zealous effort to help people live healthy, joyous, and successful lives. He has spread this message of love and true vision tirelessly throughout his life.

From early boyhood the author learned first-hand from teachers of the Ageless Wisdom. He has studied widely in world religions and philosophies. He is, in addition, an accomplished pianist, violinist, and cellist and plays many other instruments as well. His books, lectures, seminars, and music are inspiring and offer a true insight into the beauty of the Ageless Wisdom.

Other Publications by
Torkom Saraydarian

Books

The Ageless Wisdom
The Bhagavad Gita
Breakthrough to Higher Psychism
Buddha Sutra — A Dialogue with the Glorious One
Challenge for Discipleship
Christ, The Avatar of Sacrificial Love
A Commentary on Psychic Energy
Cosmic Shocks
Cosmos in Man
The Creative Fire
Dialogue with Christ
Dynamics of Success
The Flame of Beauty, Culture, Love, Joy
The Flame of the Heart
From My Heart Vol. I
Hiawatha and the Great Peace
The Hidden Glory of the Inner Man
I Was
Joy and Healing
Leadership Vol. I
Leadership Vol. II
Legend of Shamballa
The Mysteries of Willpower
New Dimensions in Healing
Olympus World Report...The Year 3000
One Hundred Names of God
Other Worlds
The Psyche and Psychism

The Psychology of Cooperation and Group Consciousness
The Purpose of Life
The Science of Becoming Oneself
The Science of Meditation
The Sense of Responsibility in Society
Thought and the Glory of Thinking
Sex, Family, and the Woman in Society
The Solar Angel
The Spring of Prosperity
Spiritual Regeneration
The Subconscious Mind and the Chalice
Symphony of the Zodiac
Talks on Agni
Triangles of Fire
Unusual Court
Woman, Torch of the Future
The Year 2000 & After

Booklets

A Daily Discipline of Worship
Cornerstones of Health
Fiery Carriage and Drugs
Five Great Mantrams of the New Age
The Hierarchy and the Plan
Inner Blooming
Mental Exercises
Nachiketas
New Beginnings
Practical Spirituality
The Psychology of Cooperation
Questioning Traveler and Karma
Saint Sergius
Synthesis

Booklets (Excerpts and Compilations)

Angels and Devas
Building Family Unity
Courage
Earthquakes and Disasters — What the Ageless
Wisdom Tells Us
First Steps Toward Freedom
Irritation — The Destructive Fire
Responsibility
Responsibility and Business
Responsibilities of Fathers
Responsibilities of Mothers
Success
Torchbearers
What to Look for in the Heart of Your Partner

Videos

The Seven Rays Interpreted
Lecture Videos by the Author

For an updated list of publications, please contact T.S.G. Publishing Foundation, Inc.

Ordering Information

Write to the publisher for additional information regarding:

— Free catalog of author's books and music tapes
— Lecture tapes and videos; complete list available
— Placement on mailing list
— New releases
— A free copy of our newsletter *Outreach*

Additional copies of ***Duties of Grandparents***
U.S. $4.00 (softcover)

Postage within U.S.A. – $1.50
Plus applicable state sales tax
International postage: contact us for rates

T.S.G. Publishing Foundation, Inc.
P. O. Box 7068
Cave Creek, AZ 85331-7068
United States of America

TEL: (602) 502-1909
FAX: (602) 502-0713
EMAIL: TSG@DOITNOW.COM

T.S.G. Publishing Foundation, Inc. is a non-profit, tax exempt organization.

Our purpose is to be a pathway for self-transformation. We offer books, audio and video tapes, classes and seminars, and home study courses based on the core values and higher principles of the Ageless Wisdom.

These fine books have been published by the generous donations of the students of the Ageless Wisdom.

Your tax deductible contributions will help us continue publishing and growing.

Our gratitude to all.